OUR TIME BY THE CLOCK

OUR TIME BY THE CLOCK

CHRISDINA NIXON

BLKDOG

www.blkdogpublishing.com

CHAPTER ONE

"**A** **clock** doesn't give a Fuck.

It will say anything.

Time doesn't need it to keep going.

It will keep moving onwards without the hands keeping pace.

The clock in here stopped days before your mother died.

When I heard you were dead I was wearing a Timex watch.

A narrow strap of leather, a gold face with no numbers.

A Christmas present.

I couldn't tell the time but it was early in the day and I heard words I would hear over and over;

"He's dead."

There was no going back and life divided into Time before and Time after you.

Everything changed after you were gone.

Stupid things.

There was never toilet paper after you died.

Nothing passed a Sell-By Date or remained forgotten at the back of a cupboard.

There was never enough money.

In a very short time there was not even a You.
Our lives became quickly rewritten and nothing resembled
Time with you in it.
All bills and demands came addressed solely to her and
Love Mom x on Christmas presents confirmed you were
gone.
Why are you smiling?
You left such a fucking mess!"

The darkness that held her father lightened and shifted
closer.

You were with your mother in the hours before you
died.
Pacing the living room of her flat, that comic-like quick-
ened walk.
She said you were disturbed…"

Catherine closed her eyes as sounds skimmed by and hit
her face in anger.
The room dismantling around her.
Her lips tasted of dirt.
Stale, rancid earth.
She knew what he was capable of.
He would bury her alive.
Catherine held up her hands.

Her words."

She fell.
Between her and the floor the body of a naked child.
Repulsed she pushed herself away.
The girl's voice reacted to Catherine's touch and for a
moment the room filled with a powerless
 living sound.

Granny Rosie's." she screamed.

Sounds fell and vanished.
Swallowed by the floor.
Cleansed by the moment.
He waited for her to speak.

"She said.
She said she felt helpless as she watched your body jerk and twist with torment.
Frightened by the meaning of the awful words you threw at her.
Descriptions of evil acts.
Then you were calm, quiet....
You promised her that all you had done was drive the car. Nothing more.
Told her you were sorry.
Swore you had not touched or harmed any of the girls.
You left.
I think I always knew you had abducted and murdered those girls."

Laughter and darkness became one.
It and Catherine both knew she was damned.

"After you were gone we ate every form of frozen and tinned meat.
Paste that came in tiny jars and hardened on bread.
Food that delivered nothing of the promise of the labels.
Powdered Mash that re-hydrated with boiling water and desserts that did likewise when whisked
 through cold milk"

Fruit gained a uniform shape and became a colour.
A treat.
Dissolved in a bowl of boiling water before bed on a Saturday night.
Quivering translucent red, or yellow sweetness that was

spooned into bowls after Sunday dinner.
On the aberrant days that their mother got up early, Peter,
David and Catherine caught a bus to
 school where they ate free dinners.
Mostly they stayed home.
As Time passed they began to hide inside the house.

"After you died we never answered the door.
Not to the well dressed, uniform or overall wearer.
Never to anyone who seemed to step back and scan the
windows for movement.
Not to anyone really.
We all lay on the kitchen floor when the headmaster
banged on the front windows and called out
each of our names."

A truancy officer became their regular visitor. Each of the
children had a favoured window to view
 his movements. They watched in silence as he again
scribbled a note and pushed it through the
 letterbox, sometimes taking a peek through the flap his
Notice had disappeared into.

"I think he knew we were in there."

Some days he would linger in his car as though trying to
wait them out. Or be lucky enough to
 catch one of them returning home. The note would in-
form Maeve that he had again visited, and
again had been unable to make contact with her. It stated
that her children, naming the three of
 school going age, had now been absent from school for all
but two days of the present term.
He emphasised the importance of the matter and stated
that to avoid further action she should
 contact him immediately.

"She never did and we left the house and the country before any court orders were enforced."

CHAPTER TWO

"**G**ranny Rosie never denied that she saw and talked to you after you died.
I never wanted you to be a ghost, but I did not want to disbelieve her either.
Part of me wishing it to be true.
Part of me knowing it was."

Her remaining children assured her that the presence was triggered by grief.
A trick.
A kind deception employed by her mind.
"Dreams, just dreams Rosie"
She dismissed what they said.
She knew her son was real.
"No one could dream someone so unhappy."
Her family ignored her behaviour, sure that given time it would pass as their mother came to terms
with the loss of her youngest child.

"**They** believed her loneliness conjured you up.
That and the unbearable reality that she would never see you again.

In the early months we were all sent to stay with her.
A fleet of on-hand grandchildren an alternative to them
having to face her.
When it was my turn I was disappointed that you chose to
remain hidden.
I still loved you then.
So much.
I pretended you had gone somewhere secret.
That nothing bad had happened.
Then I thought that maybe they couldn't tell us where you
were.
That they had all sworn a secret oath.
That you were a spy or a pirate.
A criminal in prison.
Anything was better than being dead.

Within hours of the accident we all knew you were dead."

Police had quickly put a name to the deceased.
A driving license, an address book and a Saint Christopher
medal were in the inside pocket of his
jacket.
Because of the state of the body authorities had recom-
mended that Maeve not be the one to
identify her husband's remains. Asking if it would be possi-
ble for anther close family member to
attend the mortuary.

"Uncle Chris did. He said all that was recognisable was
your sleeked black hair, the cygnet ring
you wore on your wedding finger, and the saint Christo-
pher medal that Grannie Rosie had
given you to keep you safe when you drove."

Chris cried when alone with his wife and told her that the
hair was soaked in blood and pieces of
mush that he assumed was his younger brother's brain.

Talked of how proud his brother had been of his thick hair, and from a teen had always spent hours
getting it to sit just right. How he manoeuvred the front so it appeared as though strands had fallen
free.
Chris imagined he could smell the hair oil before the sheet was lifted from his baby brother.
There were no facial features that he could say belonged to his brother.
What was shown to him was something that once had been a living person.
No one else saw the body and no attempt was made to change how he looked.
Days later a closed casket greeted his wife and family at the funeral home.

"That day we were at school.
The three of us no longer together as Peter had passed his Eleven Plus. His uniform navy blue, not
the burgundy jumper and grey blazer of Saint Joseph's that David and I still wore."

Morning break had just begun, Catherine was sat in a cloakroom when David came looking for
her. When Peter had still been at the school David never spoke to her. Her eldest brother, Peter,
had warned her not to tell anyone she was their sister.
David was nicer to her once Peter had moved on.
That morning he said the headmaster wanted to see both of them straight after break. He told his
sister to stay where she was and wait for him to come back.
As he left, so did Catherine.

"I was afraid.
Afraid I was in trouble.
I had only been in the headmaster's office twice.

First when I had a nose bleed, another girl had hit me with
her elbow whilst dancing as a butterfly
 in rehearsals for the school play.
The second.
Well, you know why.
It was your fault."

A Prefect began a performance with a loud knock on
Catherine's classroom door. Without waiting
 for a response he entered the room.
Walked straight to the teacher and handed her a note.
With his chin lifted he stood and waited whilst she read.

"Prick!
She folded the paper and in a voice I couldn't believe be-
longed to her, spat out my repugnant
 name;
*"Catherine.
Headmaster's office!"*

Catherine knew why she was being summoned, so too the
pitying eyes that escorted her walk from
 her desk and out through the door way.

"I'd brought a copy of Playboy to school."

The Prefect never spoke and Catherine followed in wor-
ried silence.
Their feet squeaking on the highly polished parquet floors.
He quickened his pace and Catherine's
 heart beat in time as she tried to keep up. Panicked that
he would arrive at the headmaster's door,
turn and reveal she wasn't there. Something else she would
have to explain. The magazine had
 been in her possession for some time.
She'd found it in the cupboard under the stairs.
Beneath the stairs was a round wooden light switch.

Smooth and shiny from the contact of many passed fingers.
It sat above the door almost touching the ceiling. A naked low watt bulb hung lifeless from a thin
platted flex.
Christmas decorations relegated from the trunk in the attic spilled from cardboard boxes and bags.
They would take no further part in festivities and waited for Time to pass.
Pushed in beside unrecognisable strips of vests and pyjamas reincarnated for domestic servitude
were four glossy porn magazines.
She had flicked the pages of each and for an unknown reason decided to keep one.
Just one.
Putting it in a new hiding place.
As though it were hers and she the one who had originally secreted it.
No one appeared to miss it or ask of it's whereabouts when the others were taken away.

"Did you even know it was gone?"

There was no moment when she decided to bring it to school.
The evening before she had taken her school bag with her under the stairs and pushed the
magazine inside the cover of a book.
When school started the following day she informed her entire class through whispers and
"pass-it-on." that at break time she had something to show them.
Something not to be missed.

"Roll up. Roll up."

Boys and girls huddled together giggling. Hands covering

mouths as they viewed what they really
did not understand.
Age wise their bodies were alien to those displayed on the
pages and none felt the embarrassment
 or unease of the association of gender. The pictures be-
fore them were grown ups and something
 they were not.
A hand reached across the coat rack and snatched the
magazine.
A teacher.
She said nothing and the others ran.
Their absence immediately titled Catherine with owner-
ship.

"I was alone.
She asked me my name.
I didn't know her.
She taught a higher year and knew both Peter and David.
They had been in her class at different times.
She motioned with her head for me to go outside and I
knew my life was over."

In the playground Catherine's crime was already currency
and any future punishment hers alone.
No one spoke to or stood near her.
Childhood guilt highly contagious.
The Red Sea parted with less determination as a pathway
opened for her to cross to the Junior play
area.
Her older brother inhabited the Senior section and she
prayed he would not hear of her infamy too
soon.
Like leaking water finding it's own level she kept moving
until voices and playing were
 background sound. The furthest edge of the playing field
her goal, where beyond the fence back
gardens with swings and washing lines and paths that led

up to houses whose occupants knew
nothing of the notoriety associated with her name.
 Sat alone on a bank beneath a mature Sycamore tree she
watched seeds helicopter to the ground.
The bank was a favoured place to play on warm dry days.
Possession of its sloped ground
 viciously fought over. On the incline friendships had come
to an end and new alliances formed.
Older children declared ownership by rite of being at the
school longer.
On days free of conflict laughter was the universal cry, and
games that had no meaning elsewhere
 came to life.
To push and be pushed.
By the last day of school before summer the grass would be
worn away from the pounding of feet
 that ran to leave smooth dirt tracks. On that day a final
Victor would emerge.
Cheered and supreme.
Not that day though.
No laughter.
No games;
No conquest;

"It was all mine.
I was truly King of the castle.
The bell rang and break time was over.
I went back to class.
My mouth filled with spit, and I gagged as I swallowed my
fear."

With practiced and gloried in movements the emissary
walked with an androgynous step. The
 weight of each footfall considered for optimum effect in
the empty corridors.
Announcing his passage through and arrival.
He knocked on the headmaster's door, opened it as bid by

the voice within and dutifully stepped
aside.
The door decisively shut behind her.
His final act of collusion.
The headmaster sat behind a large desk and Catherine
stood small before him. Her eyes seeking
anything other than his face. Behind him on a filing cabi-
net was the offending magazine.
Her accomplice and Savant.

"I can still smell and remember the feel of the pages.
I can see the cover so clearly."

Upon a high backed ornate chair a woman parted her legs
with a black and white polka dotted scarf.
One leg rose slightly towards the camera.
Her eyes reached into the lens and she pouted with lips
embossed with colour.

"From the way she sat I thought she had to be uncom-
fortable, but she appeared to be deliriously happy."

"Why did you bring that to school?" He spat, unable
to give name to the immoral.
The words seemed to flood his mouth like vomit.
His tone declared how vile the offending publication and
how righteous he.

"What did he expect me to say?"

Catherine's mother had drilled into her children the im-
portance of telling the truth. Of owning up
 when caught out in a lie. Of taking responsibility if some-
thing were smashed, broken or lost.
Honesty still brought punishment but it dissipated anger
quickly.
Stood in that small room honesty at that moment was hard

for Catherine as she could not decide
how honest to be.

"I heard myself talking.
That I had not meant to bring it to school.
That I had been playing school the night before.
That was the truth,
-sort of.
That it must have fallen into my open bag during my
game.
That I only realised that it was there at break time when I
took it out to see what it was.
Just one more lie.
Looking at his face I didn't believe my words either."

He sat with a zealous and satisfied look.
The only sound he contributed to the scene his breathing.
Daring Catherine to continue tying knots with the rope his
silence generously unfurled.
But she had no more to say, and all that remained was an
eight year old child exhaling fear.
He slowly leaned forward and informed her of the serious-
ness of her actions.
Of all the people she had let down.
Who, he emphasised, would be forever bitterly disappoint-
ed by her behaviour.
He included himself in this wronged group.
He stopped talking, took a deep breath and inflated him-
self to fill his chair.
In Catherine's mind scenarios roared and tripped over
each other to be heard.
She pictured her mother crying, her heart pierced with the
nails of Catherine's shame.
Then in the voice and manner of a spiteful child, he said
he should contact her parents.

"At the mention of you both I cried and pleaded with him

not to call you.
That I would never, at any point in my life, ever, do any-
thing wrong again.
I swore.
Crossed my heart and promised to die;
And the little prick oozed self importance.
Like a Pilate he left me in no doubt as to the depth of his
power over me.
He leaned back in his chair.
Thinking back on it now, I believe my tears and pleas
spurred the bastard on to fresh
 admonishments."

He made it clear that nothing of such an abhorrent nature
had ever occurred in his school or
anywhere near him before.
His authority convinced Catherine that she was Hell
bound and the most despicable and vile thing
 to have ever stood before him or to sully the air that sur-
rounded him.
Words continued to fly from his mouth and she felt sure
that there must be a special shelf in Hell
 for children who peddled porn and she was destined to
pass eternity there.
Abruptly he stood and told her that on this occasion he
would not ring her parents and as though he
had grown bored with her, dismissed her.

"The naked woman on the cover of the magazine contin-
ued to smile benevolently and he lied about ringing my
parents.
Just as I knew deep down that he would."

Unescorted she made her way back to her classroom.
Where, for the remainder of the day her teacher and
classmates took it in turns to ignore her.
Despite Catherine's wishes and bargains with Christ, Time

marched on and the school day came to
 an end.
All that lay before her was home and having to tell the
same lies.
On joining her brother outside the school gates she real-
ised he knew nothing as he neither teased
 or predicted her fate. To keep it that way she had to be
sure no one told him the story of his sister.
The boys had been warned to take care of their sister and
to never let her out of their sight on the
 way home from anywhere. Knowing this Catherine
moved quickly, almost running to get distance
between her, David and any danger.
David soon caught up with her. Nudging his shoulder into
her as he passed by. Her step becoming
 slower as they neared home.
Not one thought offered her hope or escape as she
watched her brother push open one of the gates
 to the back yard.
It swung and called her forward.
"Don't swing on the gates! "

"I mouthed and heard your voice inside my head.
David and I would push them and then jump on holding a
cross timber and swing out into the entry
way that ran along the back of the houses. The gates
would bounce against a wall and shake back
 and forth. We would make noises that would vibrate with
the movement. Sometimes dragging a
foot to make the gates rebound unevenly.
You had warned us not to do it.
We did whenever you weren't around.
The gates had a rough finish and splinters were common.
An injury displayed with pride the further up the gate we
were when getting it.
You and Uncle Mick made the gates one weekend shortly
after we moved to that house.

We were so proud of those gates.
Believing their vastness made our yard resemble a cavalry
fort or the Keep of an ancient castle.
 We were sure they protected us from all manner of inva-
sion and massacre.
Behind them lay a yard that was a vast concrete space of
possibilities.
Within it's boundaries we had re-enacted the Middle Ages,
Second World War, and countless
 other imaginary conflicts.
There were always stacks of timber, rusting bikes and other
things you brought home. The
 propeller from a small plane that you said you were going
to make into a clock. You told us
 different stories of how you had come by it, saying we had
imagine what you were saying in
 Black and White images.
*"The   propeller is from the plane I flew during
WWII.*
There was incoming fire, my navigator was hit.
He died instantly.
*The plane began to fall from the sky and I had to
bail out behind enemy lines.*
The plane plunging towards the ground in flames.
*After the war I followed the co-ordinates on old
maps to find the wreckage and the propeller was
 all that was left intact."*
You never made a clock from the propeller and we left the
house without it.
Or you."

Catherine stopped talking and listened.
A child's foot moved slightly.
A twitch.

"Behind the gates we were invisible.
No one could see across and we could not see out.

Unless;
We climbed to the top.
We did often in our games but also to wait in hope of see-
ing that skin-headed teenager that lived
further along.
If he walked by we called out;
"Edward Woodward!"
I don't know why, I doubt Peter or David knew either.
Obviously we thought the name of the English actor was
an insult to the sensibilities of a skin
 head.
We were terrified of him.
We wouldn't have dared to shout without the protection of
the gates.
He had never said or done anything to us, but in our imag-
inations we had cast him as our evil
 villain. Despite our rudeness he never called out or raised
his eyes to our positions.
There was also a song, a silly thing you had taught us to
sing in the car if we saw a shaved head.
When we would be almost out of sight our courage was at
it's highest and we'd sing;
Skin head, skin head over there.
What's it like to have no hair?
Is it hot or is it cold?
I don't know cos I'm not bald."

Catherine and her father sang the remembered song easily
together in the dark room. The song
pulling Time back over forty years to when only one of
them was guilty.

"I ran up the stairs to my bedroom.
My window looked out over our back yard, with views be-
yond the gates to other people's lives,
 rubbish and swings."

Catherine sat on her bed unsure how to face her parents.
She picked up a Perspex box, a steel ball
bearing was trapped inside a maze within.
She flipped the box from side-to-side and the ball rolled
and fell but never reached the freedom
 promised by the hole in the base.
No tilting or violent shaking would release the sphere from
imprisonment.
Catherine had watched her brother unwrap the puzzle for
his birthday and drop the ball through the
hole as bid by the instructions on the side of the box.
None of the family had been able to release the small shiny
object and it remained securely inside
accompanied by it's own sound hitting against the clueless
prison.
"Catherine." Her mother called, and like the ball, she
had nowhere else to go.
Goldfish swam in a bowl and condensation ran down the
kitchen window.
It was early evening but already dark outside.
She could hear the television in the sitting room where her
brothers and father were eating.

"She said the headmaster had rung.
She didn't raise her vice or appear very angry.
Said I was never to do anything like that again, and that it
was over with.
I cried and asked what would you say
"Nothing, He's going to say nothing. It's fin-
ished."
Now she sounded annoyed and turned her back on me.
True to her word she never mentioned it again.
Never even recalled as a funny story as I grew up.
How had you reacted when the headmaster rang?
Did you blame, shout or laugh with each other?
I know now you couldn't have said anything to me without
admitting it was yours.

Mom brought me into the sitting room and none of you looked at me.
I knelt on the floor at the coffee table.
There were boiled eggs with toast cut into soldiers.
Later that evening you called me. I sat on your knee and you put your arms around me. Holding
me closely, your lips against the side of my face. In a whisper you told me never to take anything
 that didn't belong to me.
I suppose I should have listened.

"The day you died David found me in my classroom. My teacher made no comment as he and I
left the room.
He was annoyed with me, asking what had I done to get us both into trouble.
When we got to the headmaster's office the door was open and he was standing waiting for us.
He appeared nervous, almost like he was afraid of us.
He said he was bringing us home, and to get our bags and coats and wait for him at his car.
"Be quick!"
On the drive home he didn't speak and we sat in the back looking at each other in silence.
Cousin Eve was waiting at the door.
The headmaster told us not to worry about school and the handover was complete.
Eve was crying.
Everyone was crying.
And you were dead.

Rosie said she knew you would not leave.
Said she was aware of you the morning after the accident."

Rosie had finally coaxed Maeve to lie down. To give in to the sleep despair
alcohol and pills offered her as temporary distance from

the moment her married life ended. She
 knew as they entered the bedroom that it was not empty,
that her dead son was there.
She was neither frightened or surprised.

"On leaving the room she heard crying.
In no doubt the sounds came from you.
Said she felt no need to turn and witness your image.
Admitted to being glad that you had come back.
Knowing that given time you would come to her.
She didn't hear or feel you again in our house.
Where were you?
Mom never told anyone if she saw you.
She never talked about you much.
She has kept no pictures or mementoes.
It almost as if she has tried to erase you.
As I grew up she answered few questions about you.
I once asked her did she miss you and she said,
"No one should look back."
 No one apart from Rosie spoke much about you over the
years.
Sometimes, with clear affection an older relative would
reminisce about some humorous event.
 The recalling of the past making them linger silently with
their thoughts.
On regaining speech they quickly changed the subject.
One aunt would whisper that Mom's silence was because.
 "She never got over him."

Rosie remained with the family for two weeks. Sharing a
bed with Catherine. Maeve slept with her
 infant son. She held the child at her side at all times, as
though his being there kept her afloat in
her new reality.

"What is there to do when you've cried for someone who
is never coming back?

You're puzzled, bewildered, but you're still hungry, still tired, still a child and grief gets boring."

The voices and sounds from the television returned.
Toys regained life, and the routine of school was briefly re-entered into.
The children fought over the same things as before and Maeve found herself once more shouting
the familiar threats.

"Our lives couldn't wait for you."

One morning, as though content that the time was now right, Rosie said that she had to leave.
That no matter how long she stayed there would always be that first night alone to be faced.
That evening she left.
Rosie was sure she would not be alone, that her son would come back to be with her.

"You were waiting for her.
"No lights." you begged.
She believed that after what had happened you did not want her to see the marks on your face.
"Don't touch me."
She said those early nights together passed in tears and silence.
"At least he wasn't alone."
One of the few things Mom ever told me about you was that you had always hated to be alone.
No grown up freedom from fear of the dark."

John never went to bed before or without Maeve, and even with her beside him the bedroom door
would be left open and a landing light switched on. Some nights he could not control his irrational

mind, sure that something evil was waiting for them to fall asleep. On these nights Maeve would
make him look into the corners of the room, just like she did with her children when shadows
scared them.
Many nights his fears refused to let him believe her and he clung to her as she held him.
Convinced there was protection in her whispered words.

"Despite your own fears you never let us climb in beside the two of you.
It didn't matter how real the fright or bad our dreams.
Like you we were drawn to her, kneeling on the floor next to her side of the bed.
The touch of her hand as she implored you;
"Ar John."
Your response never changed;
"No."
You're smiling, do you like that memory?"

Each of the children had been treated to his reaction to their night terrors. Each had been too
frightened to go back to their room and shivered from cold and fear on the landing, not wanting to
be anywhere near their father but safer with their mother beyond the wall.

"Swallowing tears and hating you."

Maeve would leave her bed and take the child back to their own bed.
Pulling the covers back and helping her child to lie down.
Placing arms at sides then drawing the sheet and blankets up to rest under a chin. Tucking the
blankets under the edge of the mattress, patting down the shape of a body, leaving an outline like
an Egyptian Mummy.

She would then lie above the covers until a voice called out
her name.
She would leave and go back to him.

"When she became really ill with stomach pains, we were
afraid she was going to die, that we
 would be left with you."

 Maeve had become unwell and her children we were not
allowed to the hospital to visit her.
Unable to determine the cause of her severe pain, she un-
derwent a massive exploratory operation,
 opening her in a straight line from her chest all the way
down her abdomen. It was discovered her
appendix had burst.
She stayed in hospital for a further seventeen days.

"Granny Rosie came to look after us.
She shared my bed.
Peter and David pushed their beds together and Sean slept
between them.
At night you remained downstairs accompanied by your
vast record collection. Silence suppressed
as 45's dropped into place on a turn table.

CHAPTER THREE

"**R**ose, Rosie."
The names everyone but you called your mother.
Mom joked that Granny Rosie knew the whereabouts of every second hand shop in the city."

She donated to the ones she thought were for the desperate. Places where clothes sat in damp
heaps, the shoes were one step away from the bin, and the volunteers looked as though they were
only there to shelter from the cold.
She had been dependant on such places, clothing herself and her children from them throughout
her early married life in Dublin.
In her early thirties, her husband was dead and the father of her youngest child was long gone.
Leaving the child without his name but stamping him with his good looks and tempting charm.
John was eleven years old when she decided to leave Ireland.
It would be her first time outside of Dublin.
Two of her older children were married and remained in

Dublin.
Four others had settled in Birmingham and that was where she made her home. Rosie would
spend fifty six years in Birmingham sounding as though she had travelled from Ireland and passed
through Holyhead earlier that day. All of the family spoke with distinct Irish accents, even John
 who had left Dublin at such a young age.
Work was plentiful at that time and she found unskilled employment in factories. She did not
bother enrolling her son in school and he found his own way. She had little idea of what he did in
those early years, he was always smartly dressed and never asked for money. He eventually found
work and worked full time with a house painter.
By the age of nineteen he had met and married Maeve.
They had one child and another on the way.
Rosie continued to work and enjoyed the luxury of being able to buy the things she wanted.
She felt she owed a debt to the run down shops and from their depressing shelves she
bought little ornaments and toys that would fit into her coat pockets. She had no use
for the objects often leaving them on the seat of the bus on her way home, or donating them in the
next shop she visited.
As time passed Second Hand almost supplanted her religion and she worshipped at Saint Martin's
 indoor rag market in the centre of town.

"It's not there anymore.
Just a big empty space.
You always hated it.
Hated that she chose things that someone else had thrown away.
Always telling her there was no need to go there.
That you were doing so well.

And loved to spend money."

The market was held all day every Friday, and until four on a Saturday afternoon. She would trawl
the second hand stalls and it was here that the regular sellers had christened her;
"Second Hand Rose."
Eventually shortening the affectionate title to Rose or Rosie.
She loved it and eventually everyone in her family called her that.

"Apart from you.
You refused, always addressing her as Mother and telling us to call her Granny Carney.
You believed the familiarity of the traders made little of her. Accusing them of mocking her but
she ignored you and revelled in the affection she saw in it."

Her last home was in the perfect location as she could walk to the rag market. Still no interest in
the newness of discount bedding and china. Not dazzled by the promise of the latest time and
effort saving domestic gadgetry.
Most times she came home empty handed content that the next foray might lead her to uncover a
find item.
Her real name was Catherine, Catherine Carney.

"At five weeks old I was christened Catherine after her."

In her late teens Catherine would live briefly with her grandmother. Dipping in and out of her life
until the old woman died aged eighty seven.
Eleven days before this night.

"Everyone felt guilty that she died here alone, but you

were here to witness whether her passing
was peaceful.

At seventeen I knew you were still coming to be with her.
The air of her flat spoiled with your presence.
You were no longer of any significance in my life and apart
from when I wondered about your part
in the murders I kept you out of my thoughts.
Aunty Julie and Uncle Chris visited her each week, both
conscious that she appeared to be waiting
for someone and anxious for them to leave.
"Does she still see him?"
"I don't think so."
I didn't tell them that I sometimes heard her voice when I
opened the front door to the flat.
I also heard something else I can't explain. Like when you
sometimes imagine your name has been
called and look around to see.
I knew that it was you."

When Catherine entered her Grandmother's flat she
moved the key in the door and made
exaggerated noises allowing the woman time to say good-
bye to her son.
Her father.
"That you?" Her grandmother would ask.
"Yeah"
Catherine always prayed he would be gone when she en-
tered the room.

"I didn't want to see you.
I would look to where I knew you had been.
Where something disturbingly you remained.
Tied to the darkness, too faint for my sight to determine.
I never doubted that you haunted her."

To Rosie there was nothing extraordinary about the rela-

tionship that continued.
She loved her son too much to let him go, although now she was the only one who wanted his
company.
"He asks about you. You could stay."
"No"

"I didn't trust you.
I felt sure that if you wanted to see me you would make it happen.
I often wondered how capable you actually were.
In life you'd liked to hear us cry.
But mostly you liked to be the one with the power to make it stop."

CHAPTER FOUR

"D*on't cry for him"*** Peter would urge when tears were hard to swallow, as he knew once their father held the key to
what scared them it would stay in his hands.
Continually turning until a new idea took hold.
Their Grandmother's house was to be demolished. Work had already begun on the vacant
buildings on her street, and each time they visited her a fresh mound of red
bricks had moved closer to her wall.
She was to be re-housed in a newly built tower block closer to the centre of town in Edgbaston.
She loved the idea that she would be the first person to call the third floor flat home.
"No one else's memories or smells."
When she moved in everything was brand new and worked.
Time had yet to dump rubbish or danger on the stairwells and no one had come with a Magic
Marker to draw cartoon penises, or scrawl the words; **Fuck** and **Cunt** across the lift doors.

"We loved the lift.
 Had pressed all the buttons and visited every floor.
Had checked to see if it would break down if we jumped
up and down, banged our feet or just lay
down as it passed from floor to floor.
We were never disturbed as when she moved in almost all
of the flats were still unoccupied. The
 landings filled with the buzz of emptiness and a fluent cold
like a underground car park.
Next to the lifts on each floor was a garbage chute."

The singular simple talent of the chute became as im-
portant as visiting their grandmother. They
would dispose of her rubbish and other items they brought
with them from home. Over time tins of
beans, an Action Man figure, bottles of milk and their ba-
by brother's shoes disappeared.
Had tested it from all of the nineteen floors.
Often two would remain on the third floor and listen as the
payload approached from the darkness
 above.
They had no interest in where the journey ended for the
waste, fascination purely in its freefall.

"When we leaned into the chute a wind thundered back
and our voices vanished."

It was a one bedroom flat, carpeted throughout, no cold
corners as electric storage heaters warmed
 her new home. Rosie loved the view through a large win-
dow out over the purpose built play area,
 the Bristol Road, St Catherine's church and her adopted
city.

"It was the last day of the move just her personnel belong-
ings, some clothes and the radiogram to

be brought to the flat."

A brand new double bed, three piece suite, kitchen table and chairs had been bought by her
 children and delivered direct to her new address 18 Crescent Tower.
They all saw the move as an opportunity to discard things she had acquired from thrift and second
hand. It was agreed that any old furniture that was deemed to be of any use was to be given to Cis.
Cis was the eldest.
An unashamed bingo addict with a captivating laugh and disregard for what others thought of her.
 She had married young to a man who passed in and out of her life.
She had had two children, who often remained in the care of their grandmother.

"Bored with helping we had gone back upstairs to play in Rosie's bedroom.
 The carpet had been lifted and we scratched our names into the floor boards with tacks.
David carved swear words.
He had a favourite that he sang.
"Bastard, bastard, bastard."
He would whisper it if he thought a grown up could hear, and spit it out with relish the rest of the
 time. When we played games his name would be Sir Bas Tarden. When an adult questioned him
 he claimed he was saying Sebastian."

High in the wall of Rosie's bedroom was a blanket cupboard. Hot water pipes ran to a copper
 cylinder and through it along the wall. It helped to hold dampness to a minimum in the old house.
 The ridiculous height of placement made it redundant for anything other than storage and

meant whatever was thrown in would probably remain.
The door had an odd eye and hook latch.
There was no handle.

"You came into the room, the door to the cupboard open.
Rising your body on your toes you
looked in to make sure it was empty.
"It's a long way to the back." You faced the opening,
moving your head as though searching
 inside.
"Like a cave."
I tried to see but it was too high.
 Peter jumped, catching the inside with his hands.
Swinging his legs up the wall, the sides of his shoes trying
to grip, but couldn't quite reach.
He fell back to the floor.
You began to tell us about people hiding out in the
cramped space during the war. Living on
rations that were thrown into them by the house owner.
Sometimes turnips,
nettles and whole weeks of stale bread. You maintained the
cupboard had once been a home in a
 cliff and long ago a house had been built to hide it. Over
time the houses crumbled but the
cupboard remained. Said for a short time as a child you
and your eight brothers and sisters plus
 granny Rosie had spent a winter in there when the roof
leaked.
We never questioned your stories as sometimes they led
the way into games where you behaved as
a parent.
Peter again jumped and you pushed him up from behind,
likewise with David, who caught the
offered hand that pulled him in. Lifted me in your arms
and placed me in the cupboard.
There was more than enough space for the three of us and
you caught each of us as we jumped out.

Helping us back in.
Peter eventually managing to haul himself up on his own.
Without warning the door shut and the darkness grew bigger and swallowed us.
David held my hand.
David never let go of my hand.
You were silent and we all knew the game, for us, was over.
I cried and begged you to let us out.
"Stop it" Peter whispered.
You made scratching sounds on the door.
Soft.
Teasing.
Like a rat moving unseen behind a wall or beneath floorboards.
Then thumping.
Louder and louder.
Hammering as though trying to get to us.
I couldn't keep the tears or sounds in.
"Don't cry for him."
"When the wrecking ball hit's the house it will smash straight through that wall." You laughed.
Then made a whoosh sound and a bang.
"Gone."
We moved closer to the back of the cupboard and heard your words as you ranted on in a sing song
voice.
A whole story emerged and excited you.
You were silent and we heard Rosie's voice in the room on the other side.
 A mother berating a child.
"Let them out.
Now" The door swung open.
David and I slide down along the wall.
I kept my head lowered not wanting my tears to be seen.
Peter refused to come out and you smiled at his defiance.
"Don't mind him."

He jumped out for her.
She was annoyed with you.
You were silent, your head bowed as she scolded you.
She brought us from the room.
Pulling the door closed she said;
" Someone should lock you away in the dark, then see how
funny it is."
"Sorry." You muttered.
 I think to her, not us.
Rosie said you sometimes just didn't know how to behave, but that you loved and always thought
 of us."

Catherine, Peter and David loved their father despite his cruelties.
They didn't forget them, keeping memories close for protection.
They did what adults count on children to do, they forgave his sins.
That evening as they mad the last drive to their grandmother's new home they sang nonsense
 songs in the car and stopped for fish and chips.
Everyone ate them sat on the floor of 19 Crescent Towers.
John carried his daughter in his arms from the car when they got home and played card games with
 them until late.
The following evening he came home from work and gave Peter and David each a toy riffle. When
 the trigger was pulled a cork shot out of the barrel and dangled on a piece of string. He snipped
the strings, propped a cushion on the sofa as a target and shouted;
"Fire!"

"Told me you had something very special for me in the car and went back outside. When you

came back you asked me what I wanted to be more than anything else in the world?
"An Indian."
In a sort of slow-motion you presented me with a Peacock feather, telling me I no longer had
pretend.
This would make me real.
"It's real. I plucked it out of his tail myself.
He was very, very angry and annoyed and swore in a nasty rude, unfriendly voice.
Stamping his feet."
You impersonated the bird.
"Waving his wings and threatening to tell all the birds in the world what I had done.
I apologised, telling him I needed it for someone very special.
My daughter Catherine.
He cheered up when he heard your name and to be nice I gave him a packet of cigars in exchange
for his fine plumage.
He asked for a light and strutted off across the field puffing on his very fine cigar.
Proud that one of his tail feathers was worth so much."
I believed you.
 I treasured it.
 I held the feather in place on my head with a hair band.
Once you sat next to me at the top of the stairs and twisted my plaits tightly around my neck,
laughing as you told me that was how to strangle an Indian squaw.
Were you tempted?"

Laughter fat with memories spun behind and in front of Catherine.
Burrowing deep within her and she whispered.

"I loved you.
Loved you despite the cruelties, regardless that an instant change was waiting.
A scream of nastiness in my face whilst I sat on your knee still tremors of laughter rippling my
 body from a story or song you had just made up about me and nonsense things.
Forgave.
Eager for fantastic stories, the igloo built outside the back door, the childish games played, your
 laughter.
Silly songs with rude words when we were in the car.
Everybody loved your laughter,
everybody loved you.
You played that part to perfection."

John loved to entertain.
Christmas, New Year.
All the ceremonies that marked his children's lives;
Christenings, Communions, Birthdays.
All days that afforded him the excuse to play the Host.

"But nothing ever happened without Uncle Mick."

 The brothers did not look at all alike. Mick was ten years older, a taller, bigger man.
A different build from a different father.
Mick had harsh worn features. His greying hair yellowed at the front from the stream of nicotine
 that had flowed up through it from he was a boy.
There appeared to be no resemblance until the delight of being together animated them both.
 Mirrored smiles, and the crease of the skin at the side of their eyes left no doubt that you were
 brothers.
Their ease of being together yelled that they were close.
It was apparent to all that Mick loved and idolised his baby

brother, who in turn worshipped him.
 Bonded in complete similarity of personality, sense of humour, likes and dislikes.
John's relationship with Mick was the closest he had with any member of his family apart from his
 mother.

"He was always there, always in our lives."

 Mick stayed with his brother every third weekend.
If there was a family event he arrived more often. He had never learned to drive and so travelled
 down from his home in Manchester by train. John and the children would collect him at New
 Street station.
He came without luggage as he kept clothes at John and Maeve's house. His only baggage cartons
 of Park Drive cigarettes that he got cheap from a friend. He also supplied them to his mother, who
 opened the packets and gave them out loose to Cis. Afraid that otherwise she'd sell them on.
Heavy smoking tainted the voices of all of the family and each rattled deep in their throats when
 they laughed.

"We were late one Friday evening getting to the station and saw Uncle Mick in a phone box. You
 told us to keep quiet as you crept in behind him and shouted; ***"you're under arrest!"***
Mick dropped the receiver, stood facing the same direction and put his hands in the air.
He remained silent and we all burst out laughing.
He turned around and glared at us.
We all got into the car without saying a word.
His silence was strange, I'd had never spent time with him when he wasn't laughing or telling
 some funny story.

When we got home and got out of the car you both re-
mained in the front seats;
"I can't believe you did that." His voice sounded
more disappointed than angry."

Mick never brought his wife with him, sometimes some of
his older children came
as they were adults but mostly he came alone.
There was no reason why his younger children could not
travel with him. They were of similar
ages to Peter, David and Catherine. When there was a
celebration other members of the family
brought their children. In truth children were never ex-
cluded from the parties and there was no
imposed bedtime.
During parties the pair of brothers performed routines that
no one ever tired of. Mick would
disappear from the house, going next door or, if it was a
celebration held at one of his other
brothers or sisters homes, it would be arranged for him to
go to one of their neighbours houses to
get ready.

"We would all wait in excitement for his return.
He never let us down.
Either through the back or front door he would make a
grand entrance.
A badly placed blonde wig, an ill fitting dress and bright
red lipstick that looked as thought it had
been slashed across his face.
Socks pulled to below his knees.
He'd walk with a pendulous swing to his hips and you'd
greet him as though he were some great
beauty. Together you sang lewd songs that we did not un-
derstand but laughed along with everyone
else. You'd touch his enormous fake breasts and he would
pull you close pushing them into your

face. Then he'd lift the hem of the dress and quickly flash his underwear.
He was aroused and intent. We would look at each other and laugh at the visible hardness.
The room would cheer.
Performance over you would play records and he would drag a man out to dance and act coy as
 though they were being suggestive.
All of the children sipped larger and lime and danced and spun on the floor as music played loud.
There would be food but I can't remember anything I ever ate."

The nights always ended the same with John strumming a guitar or beating time on it's case.
 Around him on chairs or their knees adults with voices voluble with alcohol. Cigarette smoke
enveloping them all.

"You loved to sing.
Won a silver cup once in a competition.
David uses it as an ash tray now.
The plastic base has been missing a long time and the tarnish of the silver surface obscures any
hint of you."

Children slept two and three to a bed and got up to disarray and parents, their friends, and
neighbours, aunts and uncles who coughed and held their heads in their hands but still found things
to laugh at.
There would be a big cooked breakfast, frying pan spitting grease, tea pots and cigarettes.
As a couple most weekends John and Maeve ate out. Went to fashionable nightclubs where the
stars of the day appeared in cabaret. One venue, **The Talk of The Town** was situated along the

busy road next to Saint Catherine's church. Not far from Rosie's flat.

"The three floors offer twenty hours of Bingo every day now Aunty. Cis played there on the days
she came to visit Granny Rosie and on many days that she couldn't face her.
We were babysat by Granny. She'd arrive early on a Saturday to take charge of us. Always there to
make our dinner, and always homemade chips with something else that was fried."

Her taking charge allowed Maeve time to get her hair done.
She was slim and elegant.
Perfectly outlined lips, eye shadow and clip on ear rings that matched her shoes or dress.
John dressed in fitted suits with cufflinks and a tie pin. The tie pins all bore the initial **J**.
 A pressed handkerchief folded, the tip visible in his breast pocket. They appeared to have the
 grace of a couple from a former era.
When any family of either of them came to visit from Ireland or other parts of England, they were
treated to an all expenses paid night out. Professionally taken and framed black and white
 photographs with Hawaiian backgrounds and Hawaiian palm trees. Drinks in tall glasses with
 umbrellas and garlands around the women's necks were later presented as a reminder of the good
 time.
In most of the pictures Maeve rested her head on John's shoulder and smiled contentedly. Her eyes
 telling tales of the rum and black she had drank.
Sometimes an older cousin babysat and Rosie accompanied the group. Seated the other side
 of her son and looking directly into the camera.

Mick most times completed the tableau.

"We always thought you were rich. You appeared to be a successful business man, running your
own contract cleaning firm. There were vans and men who worked for you. They came to the
parties. Sometimes with wives or girlfriends.
 I remember you and Mom on the floor of the sitting room counting money. A metal, narrow,
 padlocked box that was kept under your bed. The notes inside held in bundles with brown elastic
bands. Mom wrote the amounts you told her next to names in a note book that was also kept in the
strong box.
After you died the key to the box couldn't be found, and we watched Mom break it open with a
hammer.
There was no money inside.
A few paper clips, elastic bands and strips of material.
Mom put the material in her pocket and left the rest on the floor.
You worked hard and would be gone early in the morning.
Sometimes we didn't see you for days.
 One school holiday took my cousin, Geraldine and I to work with you. Her father, Mom's brother
 worked for you. We left in the light of an early morning in summer to go to a factory. Inside there
were no windows and the over head lights in the building made a brightness that illuminated the
 walls and created shadows that we knew were to be avoid-
ed. There was a cafeteria for the workers
with rows of tables, chairs turned upside down hung over their edges and the floor was scattered
with cigarette butts, paper and food.
On a wall there was a machine that dispensed chocolate bars, and you told us a small man lived
inside to give out the chocolate.

Warned us not to put our fingers too far into the opening
where the bars appeared because the man
 wasn't very nice.
That he hated his job and for fun would try to pull us in.
Left us coins and told us not to leave the cafeteria as you
split the men into gangs and sent them to
 clean different areas of the factory.
We fed all our money to the small man, ate his chocolate
and tried to figure how he got in.
You loved money,
you loved to spend it
and you loved to own things.
You came home with a 8mm movie camera, a projector
and a screen that pulled down like a roller
blind and folded away. There were spools of films, cartoon
features. Top Cat and The Flintstones,
all with no sound.
 And stacks of what you joked were called Blue movies.
There was one you let us watch part of. Playing it back-
wards so that the woman appeared naked
and put her clothes back on. You and Mike made up a
soundtrack with whistling, humming and
funny animal style sounds. The other films in the box were
watched late at night when we went to
 be and other couples called round."

John bought musical instruments, tape recorders, clothes,
a powerboat, water skis and portable
 television sets.
 Had a collection of expensive fountain pens. Treasured
one above all the others.
It had cost him a lot of money.
It was sleek and gleaming in black. A dart of bright colour
ran to the nib and he promised his
 children it was real gold.
Each of the pens were held cushioned in hinged cases. He
would line them out on the table and

display them like artefacts. The children gazed with their
hands held tight to their sides. Fingertips
pushed into thighs for fear they would move and touch
what they would not even breath upon.
Once when David and Catherine were alone in the house
they removed all of the pens from their
cases, eager to see their names brought to life by their
wonder.
Each scratched emptiness across the page.
None had tasted ink.

"I used one of your pens at school for awhile.
Someone took it but I didn't really care.
There were desk diaries, address books and leather bound
volumes on Economics kept behind the
leaded glass of an oak bookcase that stood too big for the
hallway between the sitting room and
kitchen."

On the obstruction all had stubbed toes, clipped a knee or
caught bruises on a limb not kept in
check as they manoeuvred by.

"We loved when it happened to you, when you knocked
into it.
In lowered voices we'd repeat your mocking words.
*"Jumped out at you did it? Wouldn't happen if
you were watching where you
were going."*
Never saw you take a book from any of those shelves.
Years later Granny told me you were illiterate, unable to
write or decipher the letters of your own
name.
No one read any of the books, and I was glad because to
me the bookcase had nothing to do with
the written word.I would sit in front of it on a stool, one of
the fancy leather bound hardbacks

propped open, my fingers moving and I could hear the sounds of the keys of a piano. I played the
most amazing music inside my head.
I had seen an electric organ in the window of a music shop in town. It was bright red with two
curved metal legs. Every time Mom and I got off at a certain bus stop I made her come and look to
 make sure it was still there. She told me it wasn't real and only there as a display.
 "Not for sale."
I had begged her to go in and ask and she told me that she had and that was how she knew.
You had gone back to Dublin with Granny and other members of your family for the funeral of
some relative and when you came back we each got presents.
I forget what the boys got.
I got the electric organ.
First I thought you had read my mind but then you told me a little bird had landed on your
 shoulder and whispered my wishes in your ear.
The notes were represented by numbers and there was a book of known tunes for me to learn. I
 became expert at Silent Night. The organ hummed when it was switched
on. David and Peter held their hands down on as many of the keys as possible and it
sounded like it was announcing a phantom. They picked the numbers off and switched their places
 so as no note corresponded to it's allotted number. But my fingers remembered Silent Night.
When next in town checked the music shop window and the display had been changed. I was glad,
as it meant you hadn't lied about the bird.

CHAPTER FIVE

"**When** I was seventeen
I knew Granny was the only person who
might know the truth of what I believed
about you.
I didn't know if she'd tell me anything and I had n idea
how to ask.
All I knew was the blatant forgetting of you made me more
curious and my mind joined the dots I
believed were there,
I didn't tell Mom I had written to Rosie asking could I go
and stay.
She replied Yes and I left.
When I got there she had recently received word from the
council about this house. It was one of a
group of specially equipped homes for the Aged.
There would be no upheaval of relocation in a new area as
it was just over the road from her flat.
 The houses were looked after by a warden who checked
on the residents daily, and if required
could do errands. Two women had come from the council
to talk to her about the offer. Advising
 her it would for safety reasons and accessibility be in her

best interests. They tried the twin virtues
of a garden and panic button as selling points."

Rosie, although no longer happy in Crescent Towers, had
no intention of leaving. Her eldest son
 Chris asked her to just go across the road with him and
look. She told she knew where the houses
were, that she passed them when she went to the bus stop
and when she went to get her hair done
on a Friday.
"I know where they are I've seen them."
 She refused to even look.
"You're wasting your time" She was not leaving..
"Panic button." She laughed
"This is my home."

"Uncle Chris asked me to talk sense to her.
I knew they would not convince her to move.
I knew what held her to a place that she hated.
You."

 Her dead son bound her to a place with filthy lifts and
dark stairwells.
The smell of neglect rushed out to greet residents as they
came up the path towards the flats. There
was no mystery now as to where the garbage shoot depos-
ited it's cargo as rats and dogs foraged
overflowing bins.
Other vermin hung around the open spaces of the play
area.
The view from Rosie's window still showed the same build-
ings, but she rarely stood now to look
out on the disrepair, neglect and reminders of what she
had lost.

"He'll find you."

I had no doubt about what you were capable of.
Rosie never hid you from me and I didn't pretend that I
was unaware you were still here.
That night I went to bed and she stayed up
She was up all that night.
I heard her mumbling.
Each time silence responded.
Deep silence.
A silence that heard her words.
There was no other sound. No ticking clock or traffic pene-
trated the air to which she spoke.
And I know it answered her.
That you answered her.
She came back to bed and said she'd think about moving.
She seemed to like the idea of a panic button but saw little
use for a garden."

Catherine's aunt May had moved into a flat further along
the landing. She had sold
all of the furniture from her house and replaced it with
new that remained in plastic covers. There
 was far too much for her two bedroom flat and most sat
stacked in the spare bedroom.
She believed her old stuff too good for her sister Cis.
She bought a small wooden table and four chairs from a
second hand shop and lived in her little
 kitchen
Everything she owned would be sold when she died and
the money divided amongst Cis' children.

"When we were young we were amazed by the way May
smoked.
To us it seemed that she didn't use her hands.
A cigarette constantly stuck to her bottom lip. The ciga-
rette remained in place even when she
coughed violently and ash fell from the tip.

Smoke was drawn to her eyes and she squinted and held
her head back at an angle."

In the darkness Catherine became her aunt and laughter
answered her pose.

"She had always been well dressed while you were still
alive.
May without makeup or her roots showing was unheard
of.
When she became an older woman she was like a cartoon
of a childless widow. A head scarf, dirty
coat, stooped shoulders and a shopping bag.
She was obsessed with being mugged and told me not to
use the underpass after dark and to;
"Mind the Blacks."

When Catherine went to stay with her grandmother, May
gave her the spare key to her mother's
flat.
Rosie loved when May had to knock
 "Thank God she can't get in."

"Alone we'd eat fish and chips and Take Away from the
"chienee" as she called it. She'd already
had her first heart attack.
 "A minor one!" She liked to remind me, but she was
no longer allowed to smoke.
She said she'd smoke from she was a child.
 Being without them made her anxious and unable to sit
still. She'd fidget and pick at the skin at
the sides of her nails until her fingers bled.
I felt so sorry for her.
What difference did it make at her age?
I didn't smoke then but began to buy Super King ciga-
rettes and we'd both smoke them together.
Some times I'd get a few cans and we'd mix them and

have larger and lime. I'd buy second hand
records in the market and we'd listen to the radiogram.
"You couldn't dance to that" She'd say but still allow
me to listen.
It became our routine. A few evenings a week we'd lock
ourselves in with a couple of drinks, a
packet of cigarettes and music that strained through the
old speaker.
We'd see May's headscarf pass the kitchen window every
morning when we ate our breakfast, the
front door unlocked so she could let herself in.
One morning there was knocking on the door before we
had got up. I saw her outline through the
glass of the front door and let her in.
Said Mick had arrived to her door during the night and
was leaving that afternoon. There was a
tension between them and I felt like they didn't want to
talk in front of me.
I hadn't seen him since before you died.
"Is he there now.?"
"Yes."
I took her key and went to her flat, my stomach tripping
with excitement, eager to spend time with
him.
I rushed in shouting his name and he answered from the
couch where he lay.
He never asked about my mother, or my brothers, how
any of them were.
He didn't even remember that there was a baby when you
died.
He'd been Sean's godfather.
Held him in his arms and posed beside you.
Christening party pictures in which he danced in a black
and white dress and your Rosie's glasses.
He told me I had grown up to be a beautiful woman and
lifted the blanket and tried to coax me in
beside him.

I realised it wasn't the contact of a niece he sought.
I left and stayed away until I knew he had left.
That would be the last time I saw him.
I spent the morning in town avoiding anywhere near New
Street Station for fear of bumping into
him. I went to my favourite second hand book stall in one
of the arcades.
Mostly that day I thought of you.
Did you both share the same secrets?
Did you covet your own children?
Did either of you act upon your desires?

**"Never came to your father's funeral. Never came
to see me. No one had heard from in years. May
said he was going up to Manchester to find his
family."** Was all Rosie said about him when
I came back that evening.
I don't know if she saw him.
We shared a bed. We said our goodnights and each shuf-
fled to find a comfortable sleeping spot. I
thought she was asleep and then her tired voice found me
in the darkness.
 **"When you went out today your Father said that
when you were little you were obsessed with
Katherine Hurley."**
My heart beat loud enough for us both to hear.
I hadn't asked her anything about you and the murders."

Rosie always knew her granddaughter believed he was still
there.
She never hid him from her.
And her son kept her informed of his daughter's thoughts.

**"Said you loved to talk about the girl with your
name."**
It was time.

What I had been waiting for.
What I knew would come.
A way to taunt me.
 To scare me.
The scurrying rat.

Chrisdina Nixon

CHAPTER SIX

"**E**ach of the murdered girls lived within a 12
mile radius of each other;
And us.
I was five years old and couldn't read many
words but could tell that the girl on the poster in the
paper shop window had nearly the same first name as me.
She spelt hers with a K.
Katherine.
When we shopped I saw her poster everywhere. She was
smiling, frozen in black and white in a
school photo.
I asked Mom what Katherine had done.
Told me the police were looking for her but didn't say
why

Catherine could not believe that someone not much older
than herself could be a wanted criminal.
Again she asked her mother why the police were after
her? Her mother answered her question by
pointing to the large letters bannering the top of the poster
and Catherine learned to read a new
word.

MISSING

The image of the missing eight year old Katherine Hurley
was everywhere. Her name repeated
throughout the days and Catherine became envious of the
girl who had done nothing more than not
 come home from school.
Strangers at the bus stop queried each other for infor-
mation as they shook heads and whistled air
 backwards into their mouths in a sigh. Their eyes falling
on Catherine
questioning could she possibly be next.

"I wondered what Katherine might be doing and how she
filled her days.
 Was it dark where she was?
 Was she frightened?
 Did she go to bed on time?
 What she ate, and who made her dinner?
 Did she still have her school uniform on?
I wondered if she saw the posters she would come home.
If she had done something wrong and was hiding She'd
been gone too long for anyone to still be
mad at her when she came back. Maybe she'd seen the
pictures and didn't like them.
Every evening on the local news the presenters would talk
about Katherine, but still no one knew
where she was or what had happened to her."

Vanished and Abducted became a tag words to stories,
and the mystery of the missing school girl
 burrowed deep and sat in Catherine's mind like a nursery
rhyme or tale.
A story that no one yet knew the ending of.
Catherine followed the story, listening every time the girl
was mentioned on the news and asking
 her mother for details from the newspaper coverage.
Catherine thought the missing girl must have a really clev-

er hiding place as even specially trained
sniffer dogs with police handlers were unable to find her.
Soldiers were called in to help with the search. Their mag-
es appeared in daily newspapers with
heavy boots and sticks that they thrashed over and back.
Catherine wished the uniformed men
would be more careful as they poked in long grass and
ditches. If Katherine was hiding they could
 hurt her.

"There'd be renewed requests for people to re-check
their sheds, back gardens and what was
 termed as out buildings if you lived on a farm, vacant lots
and premises. I had no idea what a
vacant lot or premises was and so imagined they were
places a runaway child would like to be.
The not knowing just increased my fascination.
The longer she was missing news reports dropped the the-
ory of her being a runaway."

Catherine was at her aunt's house. She and her cousin
Geraldine, who was likewise fixated with
 the disappearance, listened to a police woman being in-
terviewed on the radio. She said Katherine
 Hurley came from a loving family and had no troubles at
home. She stated that authorities now
believed that the eight year old had been snatched by an
unidentified man. That he had lured her
 into his car as she walked home from school.

"Katherine being with someone she didn't know didn't
sound that much fun and I thought maybe
I didn't want to be her anymore.
Mom held my hand tight when we shopped and told me
not to speak to strangers. Geraldine and I
were no longer allowed to play out. "

Everyone on the housing estate played out after their tea in the evenings. Geraldine and Catherine
were the same age and played together most days.
From Geraldine's front window the garages were visible and this is where everyone gathered.
The garages were allocated to houses.
Each house owned one.
Some parked their cars in them but most filed with rubbish, prams and broken toys

"Your car was always kept there and we were never allowed inside."

From the garages there was an open space of grass. A place where older kids hung out but the
garages remained the domain of the younger children.

"In the time before Katherine, on school nights, we played until dark and at weekends far later.
But when she went missing name calling and bed times became earlier.
It was unheard of for a parent to stand and watch us, but then there were nearly as many grown ups
as children, and they checked each car that drove by making sure they recognised the faces."

The number of children playing out dwindled and smug parents said that if a child was taken it was
because of carelessness.
"How could one be taken if they kept an eye on their kids?"

"Then no one played out."

Katherine's picture become smaller as she now shared the posters with the faces and names of two
other young girls.

They had been taken over one weekend hours apart.

"All three were **MISSING.**
And I wondered was Katherine glad to no longer be alone.
I can't remember either of the other girl's names or their faces.
I know one of them was wearing the same plastic Clarke's sandals that I had. It was impossible to
what colour they were from the black and white photo.
Mine were red.
I remember the other girl was laughing in her picture and there was a blurred out image of another
child at her side.
All sorts of people appeared on the television glad to speak into microphones about knowing the
missing girls.
 "lovely"
Each of them was described as ***"happy and good"***
Did being bad make me safe from abduction?
We still collected Mick at the railway station and the posters were weather worn and defaced.
Glasses drawn over the girl's eyes.
Some had red dots placed as their nipples, and words that I had no idea what they meant.
SLUT SLAG SLAPPER
Mick said the girls should have been better looked after."

The police carried out door- to- door enquiries. It was estimated that they visited over three
 thousand homes during the investigation into the girls disappearances.
They called to the home of John and Maeve on more than one occasion. John spoke to them out in
 the hallway, pulling the door closed behind him so his children could not see or hear anything that
was said.
As time went on other events headlined the News and the

girls were discussed as though they were memories.

"Even I knew they had been gone too long."

Despite the passage of time there was still a huge manhunt underway in the West Midlands.
 National news mentioned the case each evening before the sports round up. Telling the public that
the investigation was ongoing and the biggest ever in the country's history. Involving the resources
 of all the major police forces. A police spokesman would appear on screen asking for anyone with
 information to come forward, no matter how irrelevant it might seem.
Confidential was stressed.
There was a designated phone number.
One evening the attention switched to a black and white cartoon like picture of a man's face.

"It was so unreal.
We laughed when we saw it.
You laughed when we saw it.
Saying the eyes didn't belong to that face, and his lips were set in a way that couldn't be human.
Peter said anyone who looked like that had to be easy to find.
A Facial Composite became an expression we delighted in saying.
Facial Composite."

The face had been compiled from sightings of a man seen near the locations that the girls had
 vanished from.
It was claimed a man had been spotted trying to coax young girls into his car.
Fresh posters appeared, the photographs of the three girls

became smaller as the suspect's face was
 placed beside them. In some places his image replaced
theirs and it stated that he was wanted in
 connection with the abduction of three local girls. Their
names now also gone.
No one would identify the killer or killers as a result f the
photo.

"Katherine was the first to be discovered, by one of the
soldiers.
With a stick.
We all knew his name too for a time..
She was naked under brushwood
 Alone,
and long dead.
I thought it only fair that she got to go home first."

Like in life the girls were not that far from each other and
by the following evening none of them
 were MISSING.
On finding the second girl it was discovered that the third
was beneath her.
Her body pushed face first into the soft ground.
It was surmised that both bodies had been stood, or
jumped upon to force them further down into
 the damp earth.
It was widely reported in newspapers that one of the vic-
tims had been alive for many hours
 following the violent assault of her attacker.
All had been sexually assaulted.

"I hoped Katherine wasn't the one still alive."

All had been bound.
With strips torn from their clothing.
Their hands tied behind their backs and sexually assaulted.
Murdered. Bodies Dumped.

Headlines competed in sensation.
Hateful Crime of Lust.
News stories detailed what the police believed was a time
line events.
The girls were taken, two dying during the horrific as-
saults. Placed back into a car to be driven to
their graves.
Reporters asked could it be possible that one man alone
had done this, and was it thinkable that
someone was shielding him?
Coverage told that the girls had been clumsily hidden in a
place that was rarely visited or walked
upon.

"A place where you and Mom brought us every weekend."

CHAPTER SEVEN

"The Chase.
We didn't go there after Katherine was found.
The Chase was the name Peter, David and Catherine had given to the space that they did not
believe belonged so close to a big city. Not uniform commercial forestry but random growth, a
dense expense of ancient woodland. Hundreds of acres of trees running either side of a busy main
road that had been cut through the landscape. There were no rest stops or lay-bys. Nothing to delay
a journey northwards as the road granted access and speed through the Midlands.
The weather elsewhere seemed to have little influence on the Chase as it was always slightly
colder and dark.
Time of day never sure.
The seasons marked their presence by the amount of leaves on the ground.

"I never remember rain anytime we were there,
But I'm sure it must have.

We loved going there.

For us it covered Forever and belonged to us and no one else knew about it.

In all the times we played through it we never met another person, or caught the sounds of others.

You would pull up and with the engine still running we'd escape from the car.

There was no;

"Watch your sister. Don't run too far. Stay near the road." or when you'd be back to pick us up.

We didn't mind.

We'd crawl up a steep bank and out under the trees that triggered us to run, shout loudly and

usually scream.

Sounds that announced our happiness.

We played Planet of the Apes, U.F.O, Robin Hood, Nazi hunters but never Hide 'n' Seek.

A stupid game that meant keeping quiet.

And, that was a waste of the open space and our time in it."

Their voices boomed and their feet compounded the sound as branches and leaves crushed under

foot.

John and Maeve never remained for long and never joined their children.

Their baby son, Jack, would be lifted off Maeve's knee and placed on the back seat. Only then

would John switch off the engine as he and his wife changed seats.

He was teaching her to drive.

John had bought the car for her to learn to drive as he refused to let her behind the wheel of his

prized Triumph 2000. Proud of its beige seats, wooden dash and electric windows. This car put to

bed each night inside the spotless garage whilst the practice vehicle remained at the curb.

"When you'd come back from a lesson you would be driving and the car.
Bringing it to a stop where we had been dropped off earlier.
It never varied, each time we came back to the car you wouldn't be talking to each other. You
would be angry and she overly pleasant.
She'd ask what we'd done, we'd answer and the car would quickly return to silence.
 After the bodies were discovered the driving lessons moved to an abandoned airfield nearby. We
had to remain in the back whilst she drove and the you and her fought."

The lessons came to an end one Sunday evening on the forecourt of a garage when John told his wife to drive the car home.
 She refused. Not feeling confident enough to take the cat out into traffic. He told her he would sell
it if she didn't drive it home and walked away.

"Left us sitting in the car."

Maeve rang a neighbour who came and collected her and the four children.
The car remained with the keys in the ignition and true t his word John sold it.
Maeve secretly got lessons from the neighbour and passed her test on the first sitting. Leaving her
 valid license on her husbands dinner plate.
He did not congratulate her. His only comment was that she would have to get her own car.

"Not long after the bodies were found the police quickly caught and charged a man with the

abduction and murder. He also lived near us and it was revealed that he brought his children to
play on The Chase.
He said he was innocent.
That was the time Rosie had her little toe removed and I was sent to stay with her when she came
 home from hospital. Mainly so she wasn't on her own as I wasn't old enough to cook or shop for
 her.
You fussed over her and at random times each day Cis would arrive."

Cis was far taller than all of her brothers and sisters. She said she'd never been measured but had
once dated a man who stood at least six foot two, and she always joked that they saw eye-to-eye.
She towered over her husband.
As a child Catherine had long legs and her lankiness vouched that she would reach the same height
 as her aunt. Because of the similarity she gained the nick-name Cissy. Fully grown Catherine
snuck passed five foot and no further.

"Despite always giving out to Cis, Rosie gave her money. Making her promise to buy food for the
children. Rosie would ask her had they eaten anything be-fore school. And Cis would laugh and say;
"I'm not that bad of a mother."
 I loved her.
You said she was like a child only the wrong size.
"Dozy bitch." you called her, but always gave her mon-ey and made sure her children had
something for Christmas.
Rosie, you and me were watching the News when the ac-cused man was shown being taken from
the back of a car. His head bowed and covered by a blan-ket. He was handcuffed to a tall policeman

and had been charged and remanded in custody."

A police spokesman was interviewed and said;
"People will be horrified by the facts of this case."

"You began to cry and knelt with your head on Rosie's knees.
She held you so tight as if something was pulling you away from her. "

Seven months later Maeve had her own car, indicators that flicked out from either side above the
 doors. A Morris Minor, black with wine interior. She would leave her baby with a her sister-in-
law. Drop the two older boys to school and drive with Catherine to The Staffordshire Assizes.
Stanley Peakes trial was held in an 18th Century Hall.
A no nonsense cold building. Red brick that stood out from the surroundings

" We queued everyday for hours, only once did we not get in.
We did it every day for the nine days of Peakes trial.
She would go to the public gallery and I would sit in a hallway where big doors with glass panels
 swung closed and never seemed to be still.
I had to be very quiet and a man in uniform, not a police-man, some sort of curt official I suppose,
 hid a coin behind his back and asked me to guess which hand it was in. One day he and I made
shadow puppets but mostly I was bored and became very good at sitting still.
 I hated going there but we never missed a day.
Every day on our way home she bought the Newspapers to read about the proceedings and to read
what else was revealed about the; **"Sadistic Child Kill-er."**

She came out early one morning as people rushed in and out through the those doors, all talking
loudly and she said he had been found guilty.
She seemed happier. On the drive home she said she was glad we didn't have to go there anymore.
The following day he was sentenced to life in prison with no parole.
Four days later you were dead.
Fallen from a footbridge onto a busy road near your Rosie's flat.
Uncle Mick stopped coming and we moved to a rented house."

 The house was outside a village far from what was to Catherine her home in the city. It was cold
and unpleasant and they would remain there for a little under a year.
No one visited them apart from Maeve's family, and Rosie. There were two bedrooms and Catherine shared a double bed with her Mother and baby brother.

 "**I** wet the bed one night, Mom had got up but he was still asleep. I rolled him over into the
dampness as I knew Peter and David wouldn't tease a baby.
I missed you then and hated being alive without you."

Across the small sitting room was the boy's bed room. The wall paper showed silvery rocks and
Space men who spun and floated in a weird blueness. The Earth and other Planets out of their
reach.
David became more quiet and withdrawn, content to sit on the floor and organise soldiers in lines
then swipe them with a twitch of his hand. He sat cross legged and Rosie commented that he was
meant to be an Oriental tailor.

Peter believed he was Spiderman.
He collected Marvel comics and filled sketch pads with
remarkable drawings of mutated men. His
Goblin glided across pages in vivid green and purple.
His imagination his only restraint.
He spent hours on the roof of their single story home.
Scurrying across the felt of the kitchen
fighting villains and battling for truth and justice.
There was a ladder always present at the side of the house
to allow him his escape.

"I'd climb some days and run along the edge to impress
him.
Pretended he hadn't seen me.
He'd stand, no costume or mask but it didn't matter, to me
he was who he believed himself to be.
He'd sigh and say that if I wanted to play I had to be a
woman, a crying woman in need of rescue.
He always let me know I had no superpowers.
At the back of our house there were fields belonging to a
dairy farmer and an electric fence ran a
 couple of feet out from our garden boundary. He'd jump
from the roof clearing the distance,
 landing triumphantly in the grass of the field beyond.
"Jump!"
He'd shout.
And I did.
I hated that house.
You weren't there and something felt unfinished.
I planned to run away.
Thought about it for days.
Put everything I owned into cardboard boxes and realised
I had no where to go."

Within two years of her husbands death Maeve had moved
to Ireland with her children. To a small
village where she had originally come from and where her

sister and the rest of her family now
lived.
She and Rose would never meet again.
Catherine was a prolific letter writer and the two woman
conducted enquiries about each others
health and exchanged greetings through the child.
In the early years she kept in contact with most of her fa-
ther's family but as time and distance
separated them her letters became less frequent and only
then to her grandmother.
The reply would never be in the same hand as some
grandchild would pen the reply for the old
woman and add their own greetings.

"Mom talked little about you and your memory became
buried with the years.
She didn't mark the anniversary of your death or remem-
ber you in any organised way.
And I too began to forget you.
You became like a cut on the tip of my thumb.
Once the initial pain and throbbing has stopped.
It doesn't hurt .
So I forget about it until it hits against something. Provoke
it back into being and again it hurts,
more painful, and impeding everything I do. Time passes
and something reminds me about it but I
can't say when it stopped hurting.
That's what happened.
That's what you became.
As I grew older I knew there had to be reasons why she
wanted you left in the past and forgotten in
a grave."

A murmur.
Brittle sound.
Catherine could not be sure at first what she heard.
She peered at the child, alive but still and silent.

The sobbing wasn't coming from the living.

CHAPTER EIGHT

osie had suffered her first heart attack and moved
to the house over the road.
She was happy, proud of her panic button and
switches that hung on red cords like in a hospital.
The bathroom was specially adapted with handles on the
wall at the side of the toilet, the floor
was non slip and the shower had a seat that folded out
from the wall.
There was no lock on the bathroom door to enable easy
access should she fall or need assistance.
The garden was small and she made little use of it. Had
got Chris to pave over the strips of grass or
as to keep the space clean and tidy. Some days if the
weather was warm she would sit outside but
mostly she watched the sunlight from behind the glass of
her sitting room window. Her view now
of people passing by on the footpath.

"Smoking was now strictly forbidden and I no longer
bought them for her and she never asked.
She'd sit in the chair and pick at the corners of her nails

and fidget saying she thought of cigarettes
all the time.
Again her furniture had gone to Cis. Rosie managed to
hold on just onto a few personnel items
and you had made the move along with her.
Cis had changed.
I had arrived unannounced, desperate for somewhere to
stay after a relationship with a local lad I
had met whilst working in the Isle of Man had gone
wrong. I had come to join him and didn't tell
Granny how long I had been in Birmingham but Cis
guessed there was something suspicious about
my appearance and more than usual amount of luggage. I
told her the truth I had no reason to lie to
her.
"Does your granny know?"
I said not and she advised me to say nothing as they'd all
have an opinion.
"Don't say anything."
I noticed a change in her.
On the days that she came to see her mother she no longer
removed her coat and only stayed for
minutes.
Aunt May and the others accused her of being more des-
perate than ever, that at least years ago
she'd come and tidy up and visit for a few hours before she
sponged money. They never stopped
telling Rosie that the bingo halls were open for Cis to play
from early morning. They,as always,
told Rosie not to give her any money and she as had al-
ways been her way dismissed them without
even an answer. And gave it to Cis.
Cis and I were alone in the kitchen making tea she
warned me to be careful.
**"Not here because he can't leave he's here because
he can be."**
She began to tell me how although she loved you she had

always known to be wary of you and had
developed her own way of avoiding both you and Mick.
She told me you were very, very real, and
dangerous. That she'd seen you many times since your
death.
May came into the kitchen and Cis reverted to the person
they had turned her into and I realised
she played a part. That she had found safety in a guise that
meant you can't disappoint anyone
when they don't expect anything less.
 I was glad she had been something more than what they
cast her as.
During that visit Rosie asked me to take her to the ceme-
tery to put flowers on your grave.
She hadn't been there since the heart attack
I had never visited your grave in all the times that I had
been back to Birmingham."

The bus route ran near Rosie's house and they travelled
the short distance both in their own silence.
Catherine had not been to the cemetery in years, the last
time she was ten years old and they were
leaving to go and live in Ireland. Maeve had brought the
children to say goodbye to the last trace
of their father.

"When I was a child you were a different dead.
I prayed to hear you voice.
I wanted you back.
I missed you so much, cried if I thought about.
Did you notice or like the things I left on your grave?
The stupid thing I made with the note paper.
I'd copied the words off a memorial card. Wrapped the
whole thing in to protect it from the rain. I
pulled the sticky tape too tight, puckering the paper un-
derneath and the words overlapped and
made no sense.

Left it on your grave sure that somehow you could read it.
I thought it would be there forever but it
was gone the next time we went and I saw it beside the
bins with shrivelled flowers, pieces of card
and other people's discarded
The bus stop was near the gates of the cemetery and we
walked in together my arms linked
through hers.
We still hadn't spoken.
She went to a headstone and rubbed her hands across the
top.
 Kneeled and spoke to her son.
That's when I realised Rosie was illiterate too.
The name on the headstone wasn't yours.
Your grave a few plots away.
Nearby.
I could see it.
I did not tell her.
I was glad that she had never knelt at your graveside or
brought you flowers.
I knew it couldn't harm you but it made me glad.

That visit was the first time I heard your voice.
It hadn't changed.
Death taking nothing from it.
 A lyrical beautiful lilt.
You repeated my name over and over."

Catherine had woken hearing his voice. At first she
thought it was a sound left over from a dream
but it was too distinct to be inside her head.
The sound was not a surprise to her, she had been waiting
for it.
 All morning in the small room it felt as though he was fol-
lowing her.
Everything would become quiet and then a shout from
behind that would make her turn.

Rosie could hear her son and Catherine realised that the old woman sometimes ignored him.
Catherine saw the shape that lingered like cigarette smoke, but she was not ready to deal with him
and left the house.

"Every day when I walked to town I could see where your life ended.
Had been tempted to cross the footbridge and often stood close to the rise in the ground that ran
towards a step, but I never went any further, reversing my steps and walking to the underpass.
"Coward!"

Catherine looked round.
There was no one there who cared who she was and she knew it was her father.
She knew he was playing a game and stupidly accepted his challenge, stepping onto the rough
surface of the foot bridge.
She dragged her hand along the rail and came as far as she believed he had that day.
Immediately she felt an odd exhilaration as she witnessed his sight in the moments before he made
up your mind.
 Back at her grandmother's house his fingers clawed the arm of a chair as he willed her to do as he
had.
The cars speed below her in both directions, a vast span of six lanes of busy traffic entering and
 leaving the city.
She pushed her face against the cold railing and knew how easy it would be to climb over.

"I always knew it wasn't an accident. That you climbed over the rail and jumped into the on
 coming traffic."

It was an easy climb.
Catherine lifted her feet off the ground. The sound of the cars and the passing air hummed a single
 sound. A wind beat into her, it's force snatching her feelings but there was something else within
 it.
Anger.
Laughter

"You laughing.
Laughing at me.
Laughing because you still enjoyed games.
My feet hit the surface and if I had been aware of your plans for me and what we have done here
tonight, I would gladly have jumped."

She ran from the footbridge away from the direction of her grandmother and towards the centre of
town. Stopping outside St Catherine's church. A building that called to it's past. It's space on the
 pavement being squashed by a city and world that was moving on and looking for other forms of a
 Saviour.
Saint Catherine's was where her grandmother and aunt May worshipped. Not so much Rosie any
more and the priest visited her at home.

"A portioned wall of glass greeted me.
It took me a few moments to work out where the doors were."

She reached out, black handles surprisingly cold to the touch. she pushed and then pulled but the
doors would not budge or give any clue to entry.
 Inside the entrance at a table sat a middle aged man with white hair and the garb of a priest.

He watched as she again tried to get it. .
He rose without making any sign that he had seen her and came towards the other side of the glass.
Without effort he pushed and the door moved.
"Sure sign of a sinner."
Catherine's face and weight of her father's guilt questioned him.
"Not being able to open the door of a church." He smiled and returned to the table.

"I mumbled thank you and knew I had to keep going wishing to fuck I could have turned and left.
I walked down the church eager to get away from him.
I knew he was watching.
I performed all the right movements, genuflected before the altar, blessed myself and passed to the
side where votive candles burned. I made sure to put the right amount of money in the donation
box and only light the candles I had paid for.
When we were children we lit them all and felt good about all the souls whose suffering in
Purgatory we had eased.
I had little to say to God and counted to a thousand praying I had spent sufficient time in adoration.
Glanced back and he was still there.
I counted statues, the paintings of the Stations of the Cross and beams in the roof. Again I looked
back and he remained in his seat.
If I stayed any longer I was afraid he'd become suspicious.
Sins of the father discernible to him.
I knew no matter how long I stayed the priest would be waiting for me at the doorway.
He sat at the table putting slips of paper into envelopes.
"Are you visiting someone.?"

Catherine told him and he knew her grandmother. Asking how she was after her recent stay in

hospital. Said he prayed she was in good health, that he had been away visiting family and that he
would call to see her soon.

"We talked easily and he asked me where in Ireland I lived. I said the county and he asked the
name of the town.
I said it was a small place and that he would not of heard of it.
"Try me."
He immediately said he knew it.
At first I didn't believe him thinking was just being polite.
He then said a name and asked if I knew them.
I did.
Turned out he was originally from where we now live in Ireland. His family were still there
although his parents were long dead.
We carried on talking and I sat and helped him with the dates of upcoming events that he was
mailing to the congregation.
I have n idea what we talked about, but I know we laughed, we laughed a lot and I honestly think
he was trying to keep me there.
For a moment I wanted to believe that a God had heard my prayers and wanted to help.
I wanted to tell him about you.
About the girls you had killed.
Wanted him to come back to Rosie's and make you gone.
I stood and said I had to go.
Tugged the door with more force than he had used and it didn't move.
"Sometimes it sticks....Please mind yourself."
Was he aware of your presence when he visited Rosie?

"When we were at the rented house Mom had got a hard backed book in the library. A grainy
photo on the front cover of a policeman stepping through

undergrowth, over ferns and briars. It
gave the number of the road that ran through The Chase
along with the word Murders. The type
was large and the cover design gave the effect that the pa-
per had been roughly pulled to reveal the
 hidden crime scene.
She never gave the book back.
When we moved to Ireland it travelled along with us.
My cygnet ring was left behind.
 Furniture and a miniature snooker table propped against
the wall in the back bedroom, but she
 didn't forget that book.
She kept it.
Even the dust jacket remained, though the plastic began to
crack.
Tucked inside the front cover was the piece of card stating
the date she had borrowed it from the
library.
Geraldine and her family moved back to Ireland too and
she and I would try to calculate the fine
Mom would have to pay but the amount of days growing
into years made it impossible.
We used the book in games.
 We felt a sort of ownership of the tragic girls and believed
we should be in the story
somewhere.
A search had been triggered when a small girl on our es-
tate had gone missing around tea time one
evening. She couldn't be found by her distraught mother
or worried neighbours. There was an
 appeal on local radio and television. Panic that the spectre
of abduction had come to our estate
despite all the vigilance.
She was located playing in the back garden with Geraldine
both oblivious to the fuss their game
 had caused.
In the book the photos of the posters were reproduced.

There was one of the murderer's car, the
car thought to have been used to take the girls. The car
that drove them to The Chase to dispose of their bodies.
It stated in the book that despite their investigations and
repeated questioning of the convicted man
 they never able to locate where the girls had been assault-
ed or killed. Throughout the book the
police officers who had investigated the crime doubted he
had acted alone. But no evidence had
ever come to light to confirm their suspicions.
I looked at the pages in the middle of the book, black and
white photos. a man being escorted in
handcuffs into court. Another of him being lead away on
the day he was found guilty.
I had been there that day and wondered was my face
somewhere in that scene.
The last picture was taken on the day of sentencing, a pris-
on van and the angry crowd who jeered
and threw bottles as he was driven away.
He looked nothing like you.
He looked nothing like the man in the Composite.
There was a picture of the court house that we had visited
everyday, it was a backdrop to a
photograph of presiding judge
It said that Mr Justice Farnham had served 25years on the
bench. He was quoted as saying the case
 was one of the most depraved he had ever passed judge-
ment upon.
I learned things from the book that I hadn't been aware of.
Films of the girls and pornography had been found
dumped with the rubbish on an industrial site.
 The film footage was said to be explicit and sickening..
Mom saw us with the book and which was unlike her be-
came annoyed and took it.
I found it again and or a time secretly flicked through the
pages, now older and with a better
understanding.

When I read I saw mentioned places I remembered.
 Then like you it was gone.
.

I told Rosie about the priest at Saint Catherine's and what
he had said.
"You're not a sinner, nothing to be forgiven for."
She became quiet.
"He was...." She finally said it
"And I forgive him anything,
too much."
She talked in a way she never had about you and I knew
she was growing weary and tired of you.
Said she wasn't blind to things that you had done.
She told me you had never been faithful to my mother and
that she had known but come to terms
with it and that it didn't really bother her as she knew you
loved her.
"Your Mammy knew it was nothing, that he just
pulled the knickers off them" The coarseness
 of how she thought of the women was in your favour.
Described them as looking for trouble, that they knew you
were a married man.
Her story led to you being arrested one night. She said
you had been questioned a few times about
those, ***"unfortunate girls."***
They were still missing when you were arrested.
She gave you an alibi. Your mother lied for you but you
were never in any doubt that she would."

John had told his mother that if the police ever came ask-
ing questions what she was to say.
"Make mistakes in what you are saying. Pretend
you have to think. To remember."
He went on; ***" Don't be specific about times.***
Just say I always call in the evenings."
He told her it was only a lie if she gave definite times for
the days they were interested in.

Maeve was also questioned, saying she was unsure of his whereabouts for the times they asked and
that he was possibly with his mother.
Their stories only placed John for part of the night and the police wanted to know where he had
been for a number of hours early in the morning as his car had been spotted and logged in the
same area as the main suspect. He was kept in custody over night whilst their inquires checked out
his story of picking up a woman.
Some unnamed woman came forward and said she had been having a relationship with John at the
time.
They could not prove or disprove the story, and without anything concrete to connect him to the
missing girls or chief suspect, John was released without charge.

All the time Rosie talked I could see you clearly, no longer a dull sound or imagined a shape.
 Now full formed.
Visible.
Moving closer.
 Watching.
Smiling.
And winning.
That night I heard their cries and I saw terrible things and I know you made me aware of all you
 are.
I had never dreamed of them before,
they had never haunted or reached out to me in my sleep, always daytime provoked their image.
Did you take them because they were pretty or did it matter.?

Time has brought us here.
To this day that began with Rosie's funeral, a woman who

knew what you had done.
They were all there, your family. I looked at all their faces and wondered how many of them had
kept secrets about you.
No matter how long I looked down into the open ground there was no trace of you.
I'm sure beneath the green baize alongside the headstone mixed through the earth there are bones
and traces of your coffin.
I wondered how much of what was you remained beneath the ground for forty odd years?
After the funeral your niece Eve came to me and put her arms around me. As we walked from the
 cemetery I asked her did she know where Uncle Mick was.
"In Hell I hope!"
She told me that he had died recently in prison a convicted paedophile. She said she had long
suspected something about you and him, and recalled a time when she was about 17 or 18 and we
all travelled to Manchester to celebrate New Year.
I remember Mick lived in a three storey house with long landings crammed with doorways and
 rooms.
She was in one near you and you told her to shout out if he came into her room during the night.
She said my mother had been there when you said it.
Had he ever touched me?
Did you let him?
Did you?
She told me as well that she had recently found out that at one of the parties held at Uncle Chris',
 when next door changing into his drag outfit Mick had assaulted a child.
At the time no one believed her.
They choose not to believe her.
The last time I saw Rosie about a year ago she and age

had finally met and age was in command.
 All day the radio blared and the television ran through children's programmes. Voices filled the
rooms and trailed out into the hallway.
She was trying to block you out.
All that she knew to be true about you presented itself in her demeanour and she was ready to be
gone.
She said she was glad you were dead, not selfishly because she had you to herself, but because you
could no longer hurt anyone.
Showed me a clipping from a newspaper.
It's almost 45 years since the murders.
The man sentenced to life had a judicial review to try and overthrow his conviction. He was
unsuccessful.
It was reported that because of the hideous nature of his crimes Peakes had never been considered
for parole. He still protested his innocence saying the real killer was potentially still out there.
Attempts to get Peakes to name an accomplice or aid investigations with other unsolved
disappearances from that time had met with silence.
The article ended with the line; He will die behind bars.

I felt bad that I left her here with you, but I was afraid of you, and you were right.
I am a coward.
In bed one night, beneath the blankets she whispered, afraid you would overhear.
She said this wasn't how she wanted to live.
She told me she knew there were other girls that you'd picked up and partied with. Some were
listed as missing, their disappearances unsolved. Others written off and forgotten. Dismissed as
runaways. She said their bodies lay under the trees on The Chase.

I asked her about Uncle Mick.
"A bad man.
But your daddy was evil."

Her coffin buried beneath the mound of dry earth has finally given her what she wanted.
An end.
And my beginning.
I have tried all of my life to escape you. To ignore what you have done, but now I have no choice
in the matter and no God or prayers can keep you at bay."

His descriptions of what he had done became more vile as the night passed.
He has told her everything, everything he did.
The sensations that ripped through him as he felt each girl struggle.
As he gave them pain so intense their bodies froze.
Describing their final moments.
The choking sound of the girl still alive as her throat filled with mud.
He was proud and boastful, then switched to crying and asking her for forgiveness.
Father and daughter stood before each other and she looked into a face she once loved but now
loathed.

"You said it would be a long time before the council did anything with this house. A long time
until anyone else moved in and that the keys would still fit the lock.
The little girl is asleep.
 She cried when we got here.
She shook when I hit her.
You were right.
You said they were never afraid of woman.
Children don't think a woman could hurt them.

Please tell me my mother was never part of what you did.
Not a silent, willing, compliant witness.
If I let the girl go would I be able to explain?
If I leave her here will anyone find her?
if I kill her will we get away with it?
I could make a phone call to the police, go back to Ireland.
If I kill her will we get away with it?
"You can't give her back Catherine."
I can't do what you ask.

But we both know the truth.

I drown kittens once.
Put them into a plastic bag, tearing little holes and drop-
ping the bag into the mop bucket.
It was filled with water.
It took ages for the bag to fill and they kept moving.
The bag didn't sink the way I thought it would and the
sightless things squirmed and squealed.
I put my hand on top of the bag and pushed them down
further into the bucket.
There were bubbles and frantic movements.
Gasping for life.
And they fought.
Fought against what they didn't know but knew the fight
was to stay alive.
And it frightened me.
I released the bag and it popped back up, still they moved.
I got the mop and pushed them back down and held them
to the bottom of the bucket.
I hated every moment, wishing it to end.
Tipped out the bucket Tind lifted the bag.
I threw into the trees behind he house.
 I could hear sounds.
It isn't easy to kill.

The little girl is cold

I can smell that she has wet herself.
Maybe earlier.
The smell is sickening.
Old.
Her foot moved but only in response to my kick.
I hope there is no God.
I can not stand before one for judgement for what I have
done in this brightening room.
Everything in Time has led me to committing your crimes,
to this moment of being alone.
I know I am talking to myself, you have left with the life of
the nameless girl.
Following Rosie.
Death hasn't released her from you.
I know it is morning although I see a clock with the wrong
Time.

Sirkkusaga
By Kyt Wright

A saga — a long story of heroic achievement, especially a medieval prose narrative in Old Norse or a long, involved story, account, or series of incidents often named for the principal character.

Several hundred years after a world-shattering war, two of the surviving nations, the Reignweald and the Dominion, have fought themselves to a standstill, both remaining determined to control of what's left of it.

Sirki Vigsdottir, a songstress who performs under the name Freya in folk-rock group *The Harvest*, is a beautiful, self-centered woman who is fond of drink and a recovering addict to boot – not the sort of girl a boy brings home to Mother.

Following an attack from an unexpected quarter, abilities awaken within Sirki, who begins a journey of self-discovery. These new-found skills attract the attention of both the Psi, a mysterious group of telepaths headed by the fearsome Mina and an equally sinister government department – the ACG.

Sirki, learning the real truth of her origin, is dragged into plotting between the queen and the Government, finding herself in constant danger as Bren, fighting for the nation, becomes an important part of her life. As it becomes clear that her life of self-indulgence is over, Sirki wonders if her new-found powers are a blessing or a curse.

Arthur: Shadow of a God
By Richard Denham

King Arthur has fascinated the Western world for over a thousand years and yet we still know nothing more about him now than we did then. Layer upon layer of heroics and exploits have been piled upon him to the point where history, legend and myth have become hopelessly entangled.

In recent years, there has been a sort of scholarly consensus that 'the once and future king' was clearly some sort of Romano-British warlord, heroically stemming the tide of wave after wave of Saxon invaders after the end of Roman rule. But surprisingly, and no matter how much we enjoy this narrative, there is actually next-to-nothing solid to support this theory except the wishful thinking of understandably bitter contemporaries. The sources and scholarship used to support the 'real Arthur' are as much tentative guesswork and pushing 'evidence' to the extreme to fit in with this version as anything involving magic swords, wizards and dragons. Even Archaeology remains silent. Arthur is, and always has been, the square peg that refuses to fit neatly into the historians round hole.

Arthur: Shadow of a God gives a fascinating overview of Britain's lost hero and casts a light over an often-overlooked and somewhat inconvenient truth; Arthur was almost certainly not a man at all, but a god. He is linked inextricably to the world of Celtic folklore and Druidic traditions. Whereas tyrants like Nero and Caligula were men who fancied themselves gods; is it not possible that Arthur was a god we have turned into a man? Perhaps then there is a truth here. Arthur, 'The King under the Mountain'; sleeping until his return will never return, after all, because he doesn't need to. Arthur the god never left in the first place and remains as popular today as he ever was. His legend echoes in stories, films and games that are every bit as imaginative and fanciful as that which the minds of talented bards such as Taliesin and Aneirin came up with when the mists of the 'dark ages' still swirled over Britain – and perhaps that is a good thing after all, most at home in the imaginations of children and adults alike – being the Arthur his believers want him to be.

A Storm of Magic
By Ashley Laino

Being brought back from the dead is an impressive trick, even for magician Darien Burron. Now he must try and use his sleight of hand to swindle modern-day witch, Mirah, to sign her power away, or end up a tormented demon in the afterlife.

Meanwhile, sixteen-year-old Mirah is starting to lose control of her powers. After an incident at her aunt's Witchery store, Mirah is sent to a secret coven to learn to control her abilities. While away, Mirah meets up with a soft-spoken clairvoyant, a brazen storm witch, and the creator of dark magic itself. The young woman must learn to trust in herself before she loses herself entirely to the darkness that hunts her.

Weirder War Two
By Richard Denham & Michael Jecks

Did a Warner Bros. cartoon prophesize the use of the atom bomb? Did the Allies really plan to use stink bombs on the enemy? Why did the Nazis make their own version of Titanic and why were polar bear photographs appearing throughout Europe?

The Second World War was the bloodiest of all wars. Mass armies of men trudged, flew or rode from battlefields as far away as North Africa to central Europe, from India to Burma, from the Philippines to the borders of Japan. It saw the first aircraft carrier sea battle, and the indiscriminate use of terror against civilian populations in ways not seen since the Thirty Years War. Nuclear and incendiary bombs erased entire cities. V weapons brought new horror from the skies: the V1 with their hideous grumbling engines, the V2 with sudden, unexpected death. People were systematically starved: in Britain food had to be rationed because of the stranglehold of U-Boats, while in Holland the German blockage of food and fuel saw 30,000 die of starvation in the winter of 1944/5. It was a catastrophe for millions.

At a time of such enormous crisis, scientists sought ever more inventive weapons, or devices to help halt the war. Civilians were involved as never before, with women taking up new trades, proving themselves as capable as their male predecessors whether in the factories or the fields.

The stories in this book are of courage, of ingenuity, of hilarity in some cases, or of great sadness, but they are all thought-provoking - and rather weird. So whether you are interested in the last Polish cavalry charge, the Blackout Ripper, Dada, or Ghandi's attempt to stop the bloodshed, welcome to the Weirder War Two!

Click Bait
By Gillian Philip

A funny joke's a funny joke. Eddie Doolan doesn't think twice about adapting it to fit a tragic local news story and posting it on social media.

It's less of a joke when his drunken post goes viral. It stops being funny altogether when Eddie ends up jobless, friendless and ostracized by the whole town of Langburn. This isn't how he wanted to achieve fame.

Under siege from the press, and facing charges not just for the joke but for a history of abusive behavior on the internet, Eddie grows increasingly paranoid and desperate. The only people still speaking to him are Crow, a neglected kid who relies on Eddie for food and company, and Sid, the local gamekeeper's granddaughter. It's Sid who offers Eddie a refuge and an understanding ear.

But she also offers him an illegal shotgun - and as Eddie's life spirals downwards, and his efforts at redemption are thwarted at every turn, the gun starts to look like the answer to all his problems.

Burning Bridges
By Chris Bedell

They've always said that three's a crowd...

24-year-old Sasha didn't anticipate her identical twin Riley killing herself upon their reconciliation after years of estrangement. But Sasha senses an opportunity and assumes Riley's identity so she can escape her old life.

Playing Riley isn't without complications, though. Riley's had a strained relationship with her wife and stepson so Sasha must do whatever she can to make her newfound family love and accept her. If Sasha's arrangement ends, then she'll have nothing protecting her from her past. However, when one of Sasha's former clients tracks her down, Sasha must choose between her new life and the only person who cared about her.

But things are about to become even more complicated, as a third sister, Katrina, enters the scene...

Father of Storms
By Dean Jones

Imagine losing everything you loved as well as the future you'd wished for so long to come true.

Seth was born with the gift to manipulate energy. Unfortunately his skills mark him as a target for one who wishes to control everything. So began a life running from those who would seek to command him, a life that spans over a thousand years waiting for the day when all will be once again as it was.

Captured in modern day London, Seth needs the help of his companions, the Mara, to show him who he is through dreams of his past, so he can save the family he has waited so long to have. A warrior bred for battle must fight once more – but this time the battlefield is his mind. Can Seth win, or will he finally lose who he is and become the weapon of the man who started his nightmare all those years ago? *Father of Storms* is a story told through time, a tale of love and hope where there seems to be none.

www.ingramcontent.com/pod-product-compliance
Lightning Source LLC
Chambersburg PA
CBHW011922050726
47591CB00007B/2296